Book 1

Learn to Draw Animal Cartoons Pencil Drawings Step By Step

Pencil Drawing Ideas for Absolute Beginners

By Gala Publication

PUBLISHED BY:

Gala Publication

ISBN-13: 978- 1508742883
ISBN-10: 150874288X

Table Of Content :

Fox

STEP 1

STEP 2

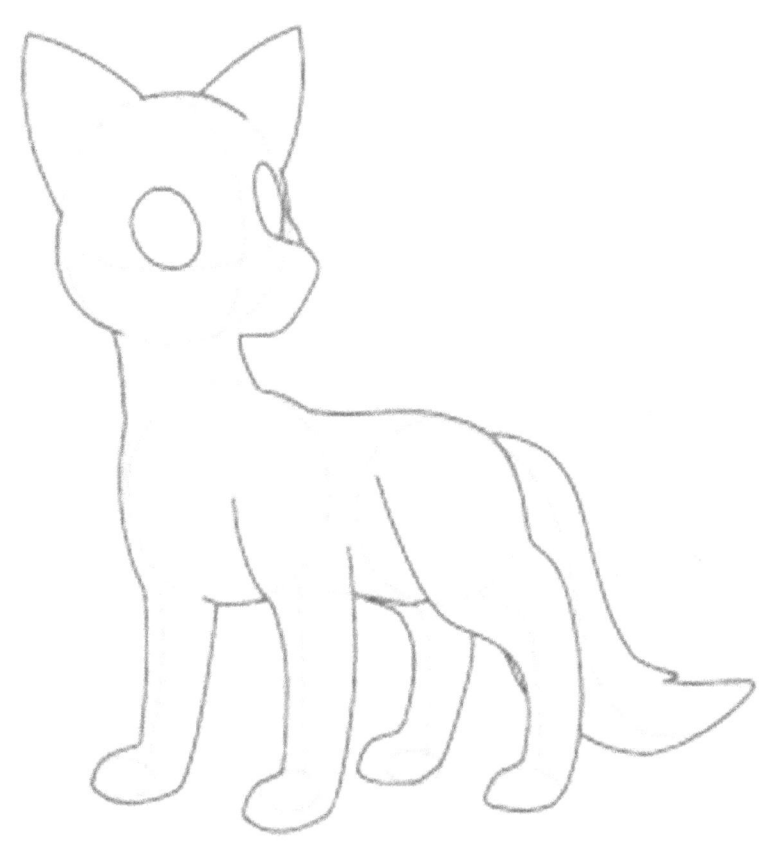

STEP 3

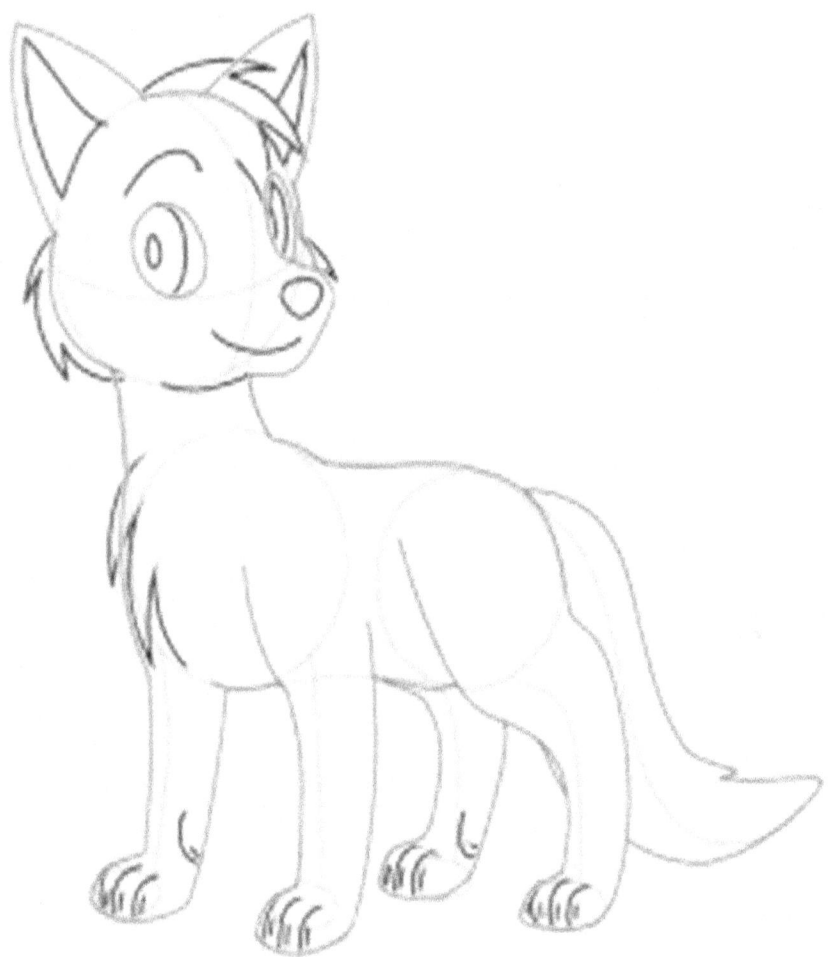

STEP 4

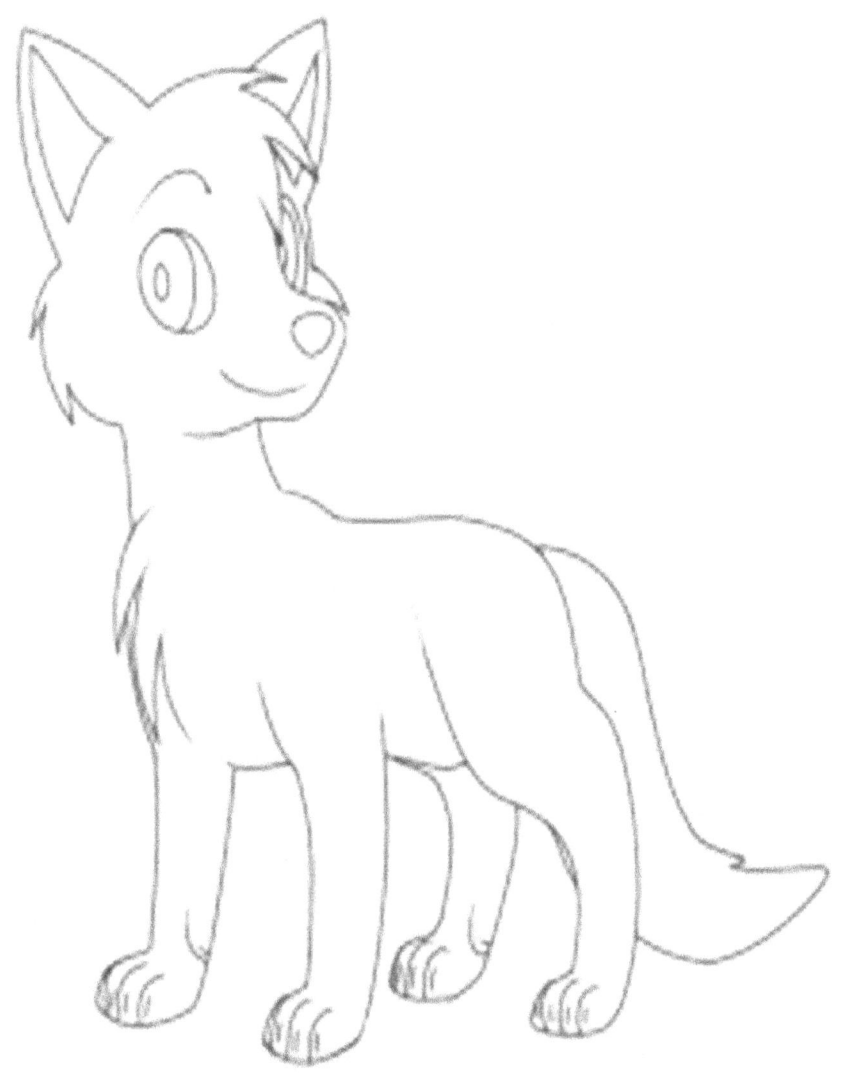

Leopard

STEP 1

STEP 2

STEP 3

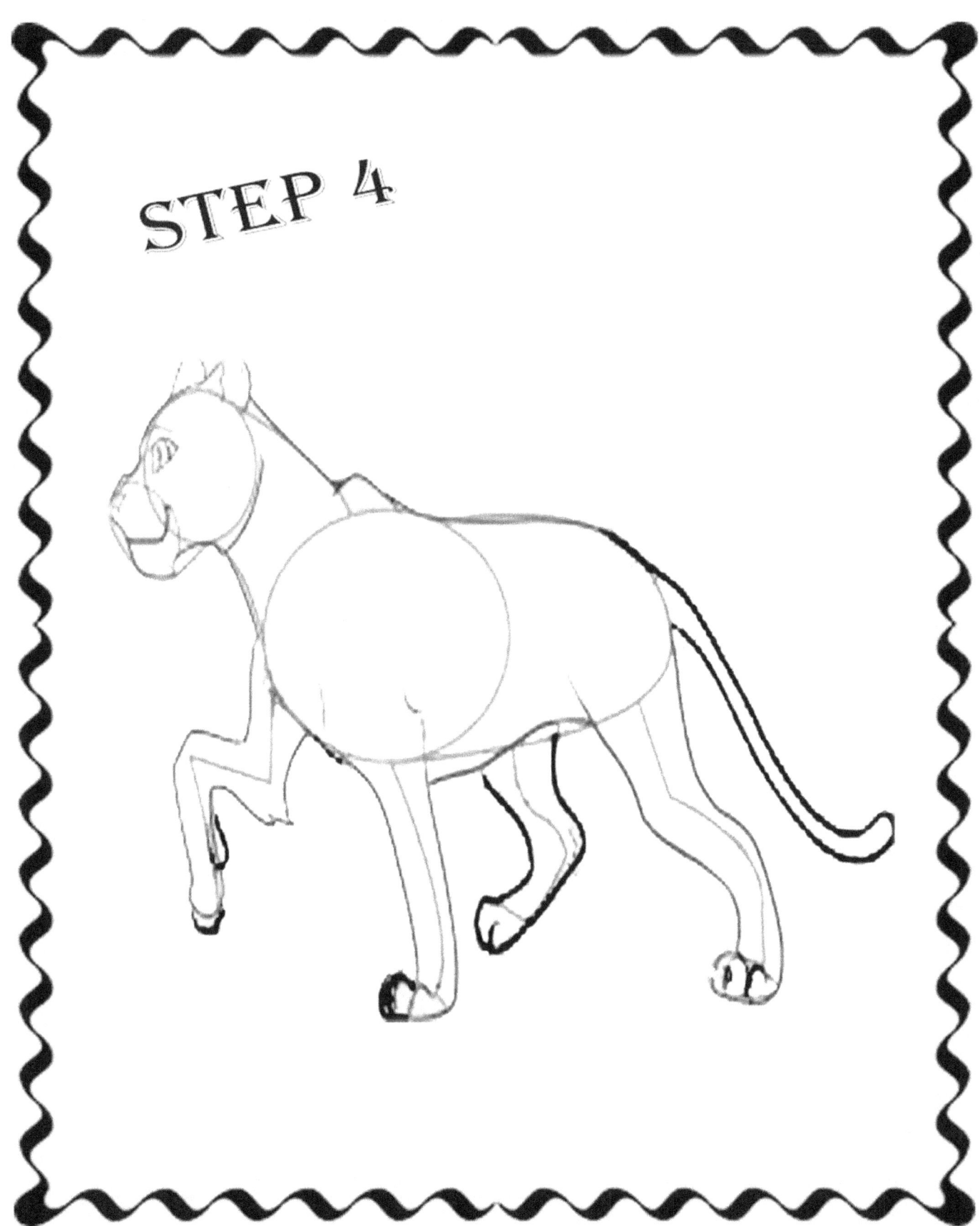

STEP 5

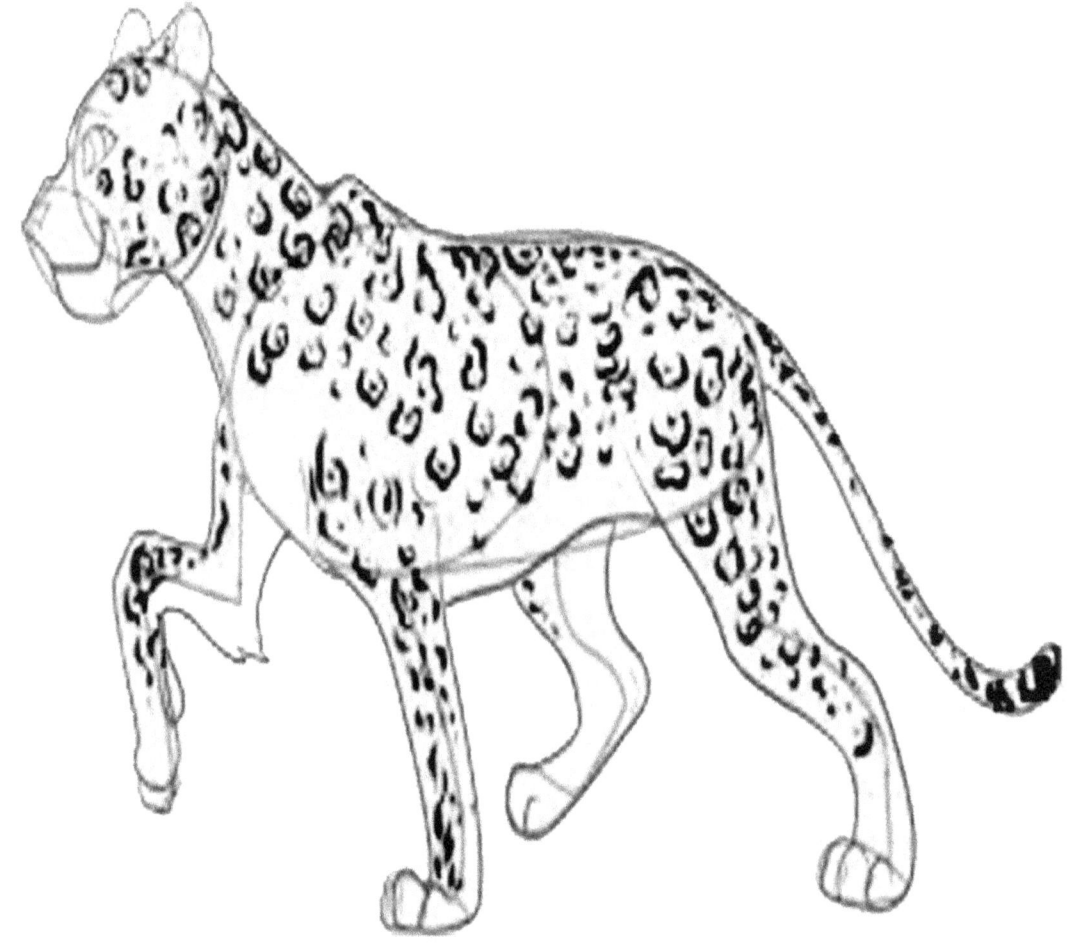

Ponies

STEP 1

STEP 2

STEP 3

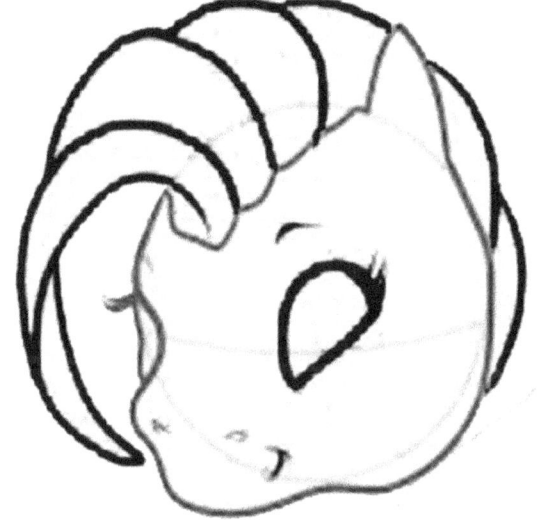

STEP 4

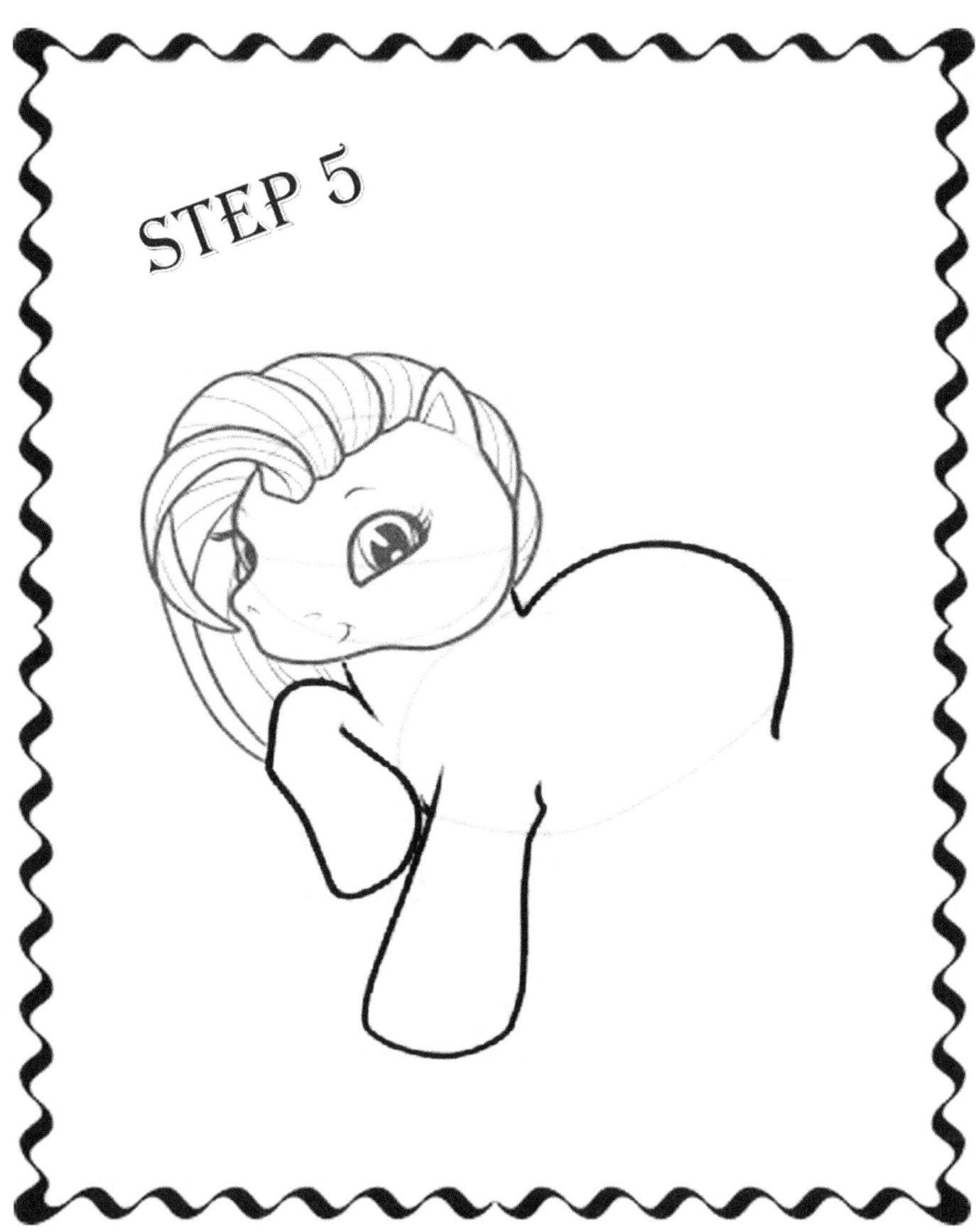

STEP 5

STEP 6

STEP 7

STEP 8

Puppy - Dog

STEP 1

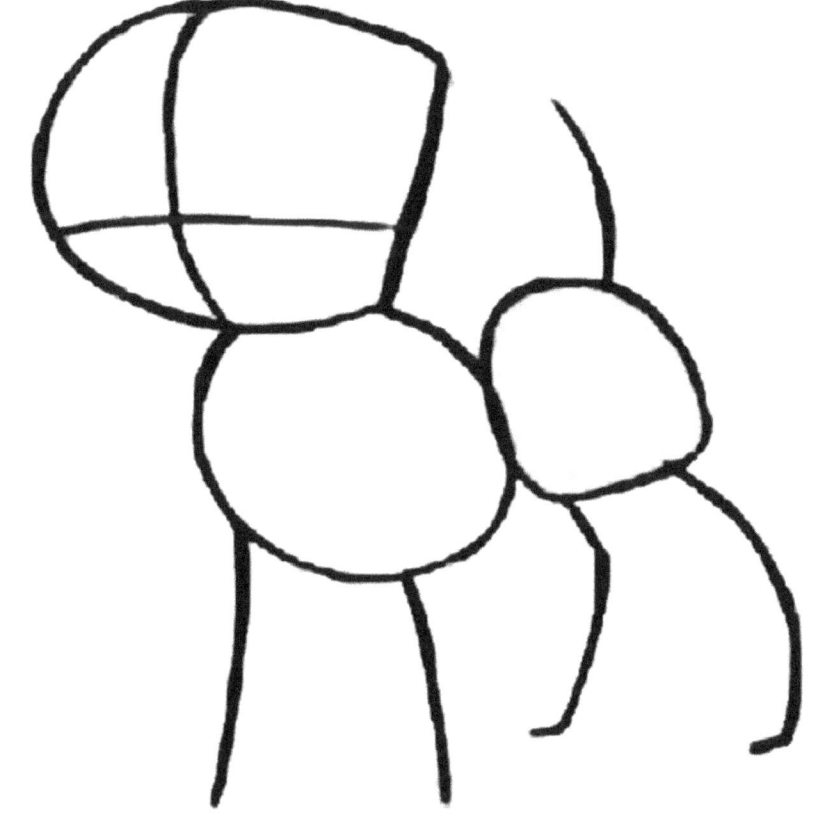

STEP 2

STEP 3

STEP 4

STEP 5

STEP 6

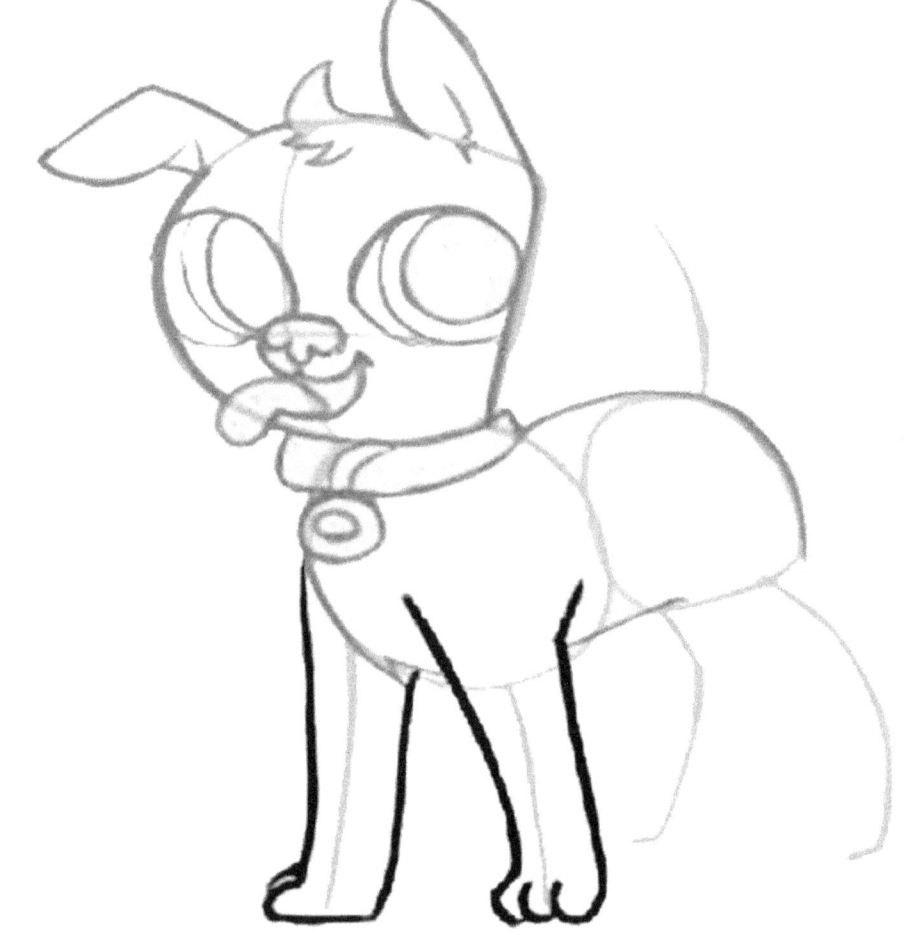

STEP 7

STEP 7

STEP 9

THE END

www.ingramcontent.com/pod-product-compliance
Lightning Source LLC
Chambersburg PA
CBHW080625180526
45168CB00007B/3056